AFTER NAMING THE ANIMALS

Other Books by Barbara Ungar:

Thrift
The Origin of the Milky Way
Charlotte Brontë, You Ruined My Life
Immortal Medusa
Save Our Ship

After Naming the ANIMALS

Barbara Ungar

THE WORD WORKS

After Naming the Animals © 2024 Barbara Louise Ungar

Reproduction
of any part of this book
in any form by any means,
electronic or mechanical,
must be with permission
in writing from
the publisher.
Address
inquiries to:
THE WORD WORKS
P.O. Box 42164
Washington, D.C. 20015
editor@wordworksbooks.org

Cover Design: Susan Pearce Design
Cover Art: Joseph Cornell, *Envelope of "Jackie Lane Cinema,"*
1964, collage, Smithsonian American Art Museum
Author photograph: Ben Marvin

Library of Congress Control Number: 2024933453
International Standard Book Number: 978-1-944585-67-9

ACKNOWLEDGMENTS

Thank you to the editors for accepting the following, often in earlier forms:

Aeolian Harp Series VII: "Worry / Don't Worry" (as "Quadruple Virgo"), "Resolutions for 2024" (as "Resolutions for 2021"), "Star Apple," "Stone Soup," "Dream Voice" (as "Dream of Myself"), and "Lonesomest George"
Atticus Review: Kabbalah Barbie" and "Thought Cloud"
Braving the Body Anthology: "AP Physics"
Blueline: "Ode to Miss Anderson"
Comstock Review: "My Head and I"
Crazyhorse: "Blue Dragon"
Cutthroat: "Luck"
Gargoyle: "In Which I Fear the Coronavirus Is All My Fault," "Peri-Apocalypse Now," "22 Extinctions in 2021," "Self-Diagnosis," and "Cruising for Seniors"
Hypertext: "On Teaching Homer for 30 Years" (as "On First Teaching Emily Wilson's Homer,") *"Ukiyo-e,"* and *"Kintsugi* for Aunt Vera"
Naugatuck River Review: "New Year's Day" and "Reclaiming Your Inner Emily Dickinson"
New Millennium: "The Last Jaguar" and "Lonesomest George"
Octopus & Other Cephalopods Anthology: "Dumbo Octopus"
Pedestal: "Dream Voice" (as "Dream of Myself") and "How to Age Gracefully"
Peaceful Dumpling: "El Zunzuncito"
Poetry Leaves: "Water Strider" (as "Trace")
Psaltery and Lyre: "Santa Barbara"
Scientific American: "Weight"
Small Orange: "Chava, the Mother of All the Living" (as "Call Me Eve")

A chapbook of the animal poems, *EDGE,* was published by Ethel Press.

Thank you to Stuart Bartow, first reader and only consort. Thank you to all who read versions of these poems or this manuscript: Sharon Bryan, Jackie Craven, Binnie Kirshenbaum, Susan Kress, and Margo Mensing. Thank you for the generous blurbs to Carlie Hoffman, Michael Meyerhofer, and Martha Silano. Special thanks to Danny Mandil for alerting me to the Madagascan Moon Moth, which began this collection; to my son, Izaak, who showed me the Blue Dragon; and to anyone else I may be forgetting who sent pictures or articles of strange creatures as inspiration. Endless thanks to Nancy White, peerless editor, publisher, and poet.

CONTENTS

    Kabbalah Barbie   5

I. SHATTERED VESSELS

    Kintsugi for Aunt Vera   9
    Weight   10
    As If   12
    In Which I Fear the Coronavirus Is All My Fault   14
    Reclaiming Your Inner Emily Dickinson   15
    Peri-Apocalypse Now   16
    Luck   18
    Ode to Miss Anderson   20
    Love in the Time of Coronavirus   21
    Self-Diagnosis   22
    Average Monkey   23
    My Head and I   25

II. CALL ME EVE

    Chava, the Mother of All the Living   29
    World's Tiniest Tarantula   30
    Minute Leaf Chameleon   32
    Bumblebee Bat   34
    Cactus Ferruginous Pygmy-Owl   36
    Blue Dragon   37
    Santa Barbara   39
    Punk Muppet   41
    Calling Blue Whales   42
    Refuge at Depth   44
    Madagascan Moon Moth   47
    El Zunzuncito   49
    22 Extinctions in 2021   52
    Lonesomest George   54
    Better Names for Polar Bears   55
    Stone Soup   56
    Water Strider   57
    The Last Jaguar   58

III. SACRED SHARDS

Resolutions for 2024	63
Star Apple	64
AP Physics	65
On Teaching Homer for 30 Years	66
How to Age Gracefully	67
Fable	68
Wild Life	69
April Journal	70
The Owl Guy	72
Minnesota Dreaming	73
Cruising for Seniors	74
New Year's Day	76
Worry/Don't Worry	77
Ukiyo-e	79
Dream Voice	80
Thought Cloud	81

Notes	85
About the Author / About the Artist	87
About The Word Works	88
Other Word Works Books	89

In memory of Stuart Allen Bartow, Jr.
(March 17, 1951 — January 23, 2024)
It was like being alive twice…

You could not have wished to be born at a better time than this, when everything has been lost.

—Simone Weil

KABBALAH BARBIE

The god you don't believe in, I don't believe in either.
—Levi Yitzhak of Berditchev

In beginning . . .
there is nothing. No-thing.
We say *Ein Sof*, Without End,
though it cannot be named
or described. If I say God,
you imagine a being like yourself,
the way you made me, a lump of plastic
molded in your image, distorted.

Before there was anything—but
if I say before, that's wrong,
too, because there was no time,
only *Ein Sof*. What spoke the word
light, and there was light,
a big (if silent) bang.
Whence we sprang, each
a shard of the Nameless
that splintered into every name.

In beginning…*bereishit*—
we have seventy interpretations
of that first word. Stories
about stories, echoing creation,
each of us an emanation
of a tenseless verb.

Language entangled with
creation: each separate
being, split off from *Ein Sof*,
speaks its name but must,
in ending, return to the Nameless.

So let me tell you a story, before
bed, my pretty little head not much
emptier than yours.
                      What am I?
A toy, a doll, frail.
A mouthpiece
for a child.
                What are you?

I.
SHATTERED VESSELS

KINTSUGI FOR AUNT VERA

In that wee hour when the cats go mad
and carom around the house, a crash.
My father's WWII picture, pretty
as a girl in drag, unhurt; his sisters Bea
and Clara also intact—but on the floor,
handle broken, Aunt Vera's cup.

It lived on the shelf beside the sink
with my mother's single houseplant, ivy,
twining round. They kept it, like all
Vera's pots, intact for sixty-odd years.
In my careless wake, this cherished cup,
two marriages, and a sky-blue bowl,
Vera's wedding gift. I gave it away
to the single mother who rented our house
when we took off around the world
because she said, *It looks like heaven.*

Vera herself, who looked like Dad
in drag, visited me the night she died.
On a motorbike, in a leather mini-
skirt and orange lipstick, she kissed
me on the mouth. When I woke,

she was gone. Could I ship this cup
to Japan? Surely someone closer knows
how to mend precious pottery with gold
to make it even more exquisite—
the lost bowl shining with all the shades
of heaven. I balance the three pieces
of the broken arch in place with a spell,
and Vera, who loved opera and throwing
pots, I conjure, with the perfect bowl
she made me that I couldn't keep.

WEIGHT

1. Homo Sapiens

We think the world belongs to us
but scientists have weighed life
on Earth, which turns out to be

mostly trees. Only one-hundredth
of the living swim the seven seas.
One-eighth are buried: bacteria.

Underground bacteria weigh more
than a thousand times more than us.
Even worms outweigh us, three to one.

So does the lowly virus.
Humans comprise a mere hundredth
of a hundredth of the living, .01%.

Yet we have paved the earth with chicken bones.
Weep into your soup: under a third of birds
fly free—the rest, poultry.

Garden turned feedlot
and slaughterhouse—we, *Homo sapiens*,
one-third of all mammals, keep

almost two-thirds to eat, mostly cow
and pig. Only four percent left
for all wild animals, elephant to shrew.

Half Earth's creatures
have vanished in the last half century
while we've redoubled.

Even half-gone, plants outweigh us
seventy-five hundred to one.

2. The Other Four Percent

I let the cat out—
I felt the cat
hunkered in her fur

eyes bright in the dark
amidst all the wild things
crouched in their night

Tyger to mice
the tiny remnant left
each one fighting for its life.

AS IF

We cannot save a single light-
second. Daylight always
plunging into night,
winging past us into space,

the only constant. Everything
spinning around and inside us.
My son says, *Did you know
we have face mites that come out*

at night and mate on our faces?
We cannot even count the ants
or name all the animals
before we wipe them out.

Daylight doesn't need saving.
We need daylight to save
us from our night terrors, singing
its steady song of the sun.

Where would we stash it,
in jars or banks? The rich
would steal endless summer
days from the poor, huddled

like penguins in arctic night.
One day before spring, this little
clutch of light, how soon
it will change colors and escape

into the past, where so many
others rustle forgotten
despite all our tricks with clocks
and rocket ships. When

we asked our mother's mother
how she was, in the home
where she no longer knew us,
she said, *The days pass very pleasantly*

and the food is delicious.

IN WHICH I FEAR THE CORONAVIRUS IS ALL MY FAULT

I thought words might help, teaching Eco-lit:
I started out gently, with a *Green* reader,
but it was out of date. *The Norton Anthology
of Nature Writing* didn't suit. We read *Half-
Earth*, then *The Sixth Extinction*; I mentioned
The Uninhabitable Earth as way too scary,
so of course the class wanted to read that.
We began:
        It is worse, much worse than you think.

We were only a few weeks in, up to the chapters
in "Elements of Chaos" called "Plagues
of Warming" and "Economic Collapse"
when the stock market crashed, and pandemic
shut our school, which sent them packing.
All of us panicking together online,
I posted:
        How often does your course work get this real?

Suddenly, I was afraid, like when I had to quit
teaching Satan in Literature because weird
shit began to happen: was I drawing evil?
When *Doctor Faustus* was first performed,
the audience thought they saw an extra
body onstage, and, fearing Marlowe's words
spoken by the actor playing Faust had conjured

Lucifer himself, the theatre emptied in terror.

RECLAIMING YOUR INNER EMILY DICKINSON

So much simpler now, with everything
shut down. You never have to go out
again. You can stay home and garden,
play piano and bake.

Stay up all night writing
poems and letters. Just think,
no more career, commute,
open mics. If you want,

you can wear all white, send
friends rare flowers or dead
bees with gnomic notes.

Become a neighborhood myth.
You have two cats already.
When anyone comes over,

hide.

PERI-APOCALYPSE NOW

I'm watching *The Birds*
for comfort. Bodega Bay
rocks me back to childhood,

the simple boats and cars,
the rural coast. In DuMaurier's tale,
there's no love story, just a lone

man's existential last stand.
Hitchcock gives us hope: the silver
car threading its way down the bird-

infested California coast, with God-
lighting slanting through the clouds.
In reality, Hitch kept trying

to force his bulk on Tippi.
Rebuffed, he hurled live birds
at her for a week to film

the *Don't-go-up-the-stairs* scene.
When she asked why her character
would do something so mad, he said,

Because I told you to. He wrecked
her career. Made her immortal.
Hitch had visited Monterey Bay:

thousands of sooty shearwaters
really did run amok, crashing
into cars and windows, vomiting

anchovies poisoned by toxic algae.
But fuck reality, back to the movie:
How come no one ever thinks to put on

a helmet, gloves, goggles, or even
a soup pot over their head? Crawl
under the bed and pad yourself

with pillows. Get a broom or bat
and whirl like a dervish. No, they just
wait in fetching attitudes, faces and legs

exposed to the predatory beaks.
I never look at the farmer's pecked-out
sockets. Once as a child was enough—

I know just when to shut my eyes.

LUCK

In Saturday school they showed us
    black-and-white footage
        of skeletons barely clothed in skin
            bulldozed into pits.

I was lucky to be here
    in Minnesota, *Mni-sota*, muddy water,
        land of 10,000 lakes

where I learned to swim
    skate and ski among the nice
        Scandinavians who, as a child, I thought
            had always lived there.

My grandparents' luck led them from Hungary
    to Cleveland, not Palestine.
        The rest, Auschwitz.

In Ramsey Jr. High, named for an Indian-killer,
    I never ate in the lunchroom, where cops
        with German shepherds
            patrolled for race fights.

After school, I feared the Catholic girls
    with their plaid pleated skirts and white lipstick,
        cigarettes and crucifixes.

Columbus's ship first approached here
    the year they booted us from Spain. He had a Jew
        on board speak Hebrew to the Taíno,
            thinking he'd found the Lost Tribe.

They never taught us that in school
    or that Lincoln had hanged
        the Dakota 38 the very week
            of the Emancipation Proclamation

or that Fort Snelling out by the airport
        had held the starved Dakota
                until they revolted

or that the Final Solution
        had been cribbed from us, the US.

After 9/11 most Americans were shocked,
        shocked to learn what we
                had always known—

from the Shoah to the Nakbah to Minnesota,
        where on earth is not ploughed
                with someone else's bones?

ODE TO MISS ANDERSON

I have spread my dreams under your feet...
—Yeats

Decades later, Shelley called
to say they'd found her body
in a lake. Miss Anderson,
who saw us, saw we could write—

The thousand-mile gaze
in her bruise-blue eyes
as she glides across the room
in a ballerina's bourrée,

her wry distant half-smile
as she blows our tween minds
with "Silent Snow, Secret Snow"
and *The Catcher in the Rye.*

She recites "He Wishes for the Cloths
of Heaven" from a hand-
calligraphied scroll, and
we're mesmerized—
                    Oh, Miss Anderson!

How we loved you, and love you
still, though you left us no note,
just your purse and keys
locked inside your car.

LOVE IN THE TIME OF CORONAVIRUS

California's burning. He's impervious.
He's eighteen. They met on Insta. Now
he has to fly into the sacred bleeding heart
of Los Angeles, though the sky be orange

and the air hot ash. He feels no fear.
He'll wear two masks. Puck draws them, from Ghana
and Russia, to reenact the drama.
Let it not be Romeo and Juliet *(please)*

but a comedy ending in the right
arms at last. I am dry chaff, winnowed away.
Let him find fertile ground in which to grow.
On the very last day, amidst the flames,
there will somewhere be young people awe-
struck making love for the very first time.

SELF-DIAGNOSIS

My agoraphobia is growing, along with
enochlophobia, fear of crowds or mobs.

I've got gerascophobia, fear of growing old,
and rhytiphobia, fear of wrinkles, though

I'm getting used to them. After two divorces,
I admit to gamophobia, fear of marriage,

and liticaphobia, fear of lawsuits.
Arrhenophobia, hominophobia,

androphobia—so many names for fear
of men—seems only natural for a woman,

along with virginitiphobia, fear of rape;
as well as hoplophobia, fear of firearms;

atomosophobia, fear of atomic explosions;
and nucleomituphobia, fear of nuclear weapons.

Doesn't everyone have those? I was born
with xerophobia, fear of dryness, preferring

water nearby. The drought out West terrifies.
My thermophobia, fear of heat, is soaring

with the thermometer. So's my politicophobia,
fear and hatred of politicians. Like any poet, I suffer

from atelophobia, fear of imperfection, and athaz-
agoraphobia, fear of being forgotten or ignored.

AVERAGE MONKEY

> *We are just an average breed of monkeys on a minor planet*
> *of a very average star. But we can understand the Universe.*
> —Stephen Hawking

1.

Remember seaglass?
Sandwiches in waxed paper?

A seahorse twines its delicate tail
around a pink plastic Q-tip.

We've made a billion elephants'
worth of plastic. *Plastikos,* pliable

from *plassein,* to mold. Our detritus
descried in the deepest bellies

of lanternfish, rakery beacon-lamps,
stout sawpalates, scaly dragonfish.

When my father began to hallucinate
he saw heads in the dishwasher and cupboards.

I know they aren't real, he said,
but sometimes I wonder what they like to eat.

2.

What to do with this dread?
Take the long view:

                Kalpas…
                              unimaginable eons…

The void
        O

            a mouth exhaling
                        first a universe

ultimately
        nothing.

Everything that feels so important to you
isn't really—

            each atom
                    9,999 parts

empty space,
        one part

                vibrating
                      energy.

Things exist
        but they are not real.

MY HEAD AND I

> *At what precise moment does an individual stop being who he thinks he is? Cut off my arm. I say, "Me and my arm."...[But] if you cut off my head...would I say, "Me and my head" or "Me and my body"? What right has my head to call itself me? What right?*
> —Trelkovksy in The Tenant

The sea slug *elysia marginata*'s
a lovely celadon with black and white spots.
While lizards have breakage planes so they can
self-amputate their tails to escape,
these sea slugs have breakage planes
on their necks, so they can self-guillotine.

If we lose our heads, no body survives,
though the Tower is said to be haunted
by Ann Boleyn carrying her brave head
and here the Headless Horseman's said to ride.

The slug's head looks like a tiny green giraffe's,
the body a folded philodrendron leaf.
The jagged neck edge smooths in a day
and the head begins to inch on its own,
bowing to touch its old body tenderly
with amber horns as if in farewell
the way elephants mourn their dead
with eloquent trunks. The black-edged
leaf body quivers and closes:
the heart keeps beating there
for months until it decomposes.

A gland in the slug's head stores
chloroplasts from algae to keep it alive
by photosynthesis, while a new body
grows like a leaf from the cut neck.
The new heart starts beating in a week.

Long ago in a dream I removed my head
in a bathroom stall and hung it like a purse
by its long brown hair from a hook on the door.
When I emerged, I carefully balanced my head
on my neck till I could look in the mirror
and fix it with a hatpin, hoping no one would notice.

II.
CALL ME EVE

CHAVA, THE MOTHER OF ALL THE LIVING

at the end
as in beginning
after naming the animals

we banish ourselves
from the garden
so many names

so many tongues
all of them
meaning

Goodbye

meaning
all of them
so many tongues

so many names
from the garden
we banish ourselves

after naming the animals
as in beginning
at the end

WORLD'S TINIEST TARANTULA
(Microhexura montivaga)

Who wants to save the tarantulas?
Who even knows these exist?
Small as BBs, hidden
under emerald moss,

Spruce-fir Moss Spiders live
high up in the Great Smokey
Mountains. Their moss is drying
out, their ancient forests destroyed

by an invader from Europe,
the Woolly Adelgid. What little I knew
of tarantulas came from Dr. No,
the first James Bond film we saw

at the mall one Christmas. Sean Connery's
arachnaphobia impressed me as much
as Ursula Andress rising from the sea
in a white bikini did my father and brother.

In a black bikini in the Bahamas,
the first time I saw a tarantula live,
I screamed. Our landlord laughed
and picked it up gently,

Monkey-faced Spider won't hurt you.
The way the local diving boys
laughed at our fear of sharks,
You just punch 'em in the nose.

We had just seen Jaws. Later
we laughed at their fear
of walking the mean streets
of New York, *Don't you get shot?*

A Brit who'd survived the blitz
came with us on the mail boat
to Eleuthera, with just a shoulder-bag
holding her favorite biscuits and tea

and two swimsuits. All day
she floated in the cerulean,
face turned toward the horizon,
while her spare suit dried on the line.

MINUTE LEAF CHAMELEON
(Brookesia minima)

Looking like
lichen on thin
branches they

sleep big as
your thumb
nail if threatened

drop to leaf
litter and play dead
twig where they

forage for fruit
flies. Courting he
circles her nodding

and rocking for
days till she makes
up her tiny mind:

jerking side to
side she rejects
him or he mounts

her back she
carries him until
that night they make

it in their small
way. A month
later she'll lay two

eggs among the
leaves where they'll
hatch in three

months as long as
we let the ever
shrinking ever

green rain
forest of
Madagascar be.

BUMBLEBEE BAT
(Craseonycteris thonglongyai)

Rumors of trouble in the hinterlands.
It was still Burma then. (First marriage.)

We'd fled domesticity to hop-
scotch across the Pacific. So hot

I staggered under a parasol from stupa
to stupa, trapped on the tourist trail,

while Kitti Thonglongya, author of
Bats and Bats' Parasites of Thailand,

dropped from a heart attack. I'd never
see Kitti's Hog-nosed Bats, the lone

survivors of the family he discovered
and tried to save, *Craseonycteridae*,

thirty-three million years old.
Bats small as bumblebees, they fly

at dawn & dusk, to feed half an hour
in the tops of bamboo groves.

Otherwise they roost deep inside cool
limestone caves in a state of torpor.

Do they dream? With their piggy snouts,
big ears, and tiny eyes hidden in fur,

they seem creatures from a dream.
They have thumbs with claws

and uropatagium, webbed hind legs.
Mini-copters, they hover. The smallest

mammal, each weighs less than a penny.
She bears a single pup a year, latched

to her nipple when she hunts, or
left behind in one of forty caves.

All the usual threats, plus Buddhist
monks burning incense while meditating

or junkies hiding for a fix in their caves,
and the clamor of tourists like me.

CACTUS FERRUGINOUS PYGMY-OWL
(Glaucidium brasilianum cactorum)

There are still a few left—

Owls the size of bluebirds
   Owls that fit in the palm of your hand

Owls with eyes on the back of their head
   false eyes of darker feathers to fool
     raccoons Cooper's hawks bullsnakes

Owls of the wild Sonoran Desert

Owl eyes and ears a hundred times
   more sensitive than ours

Owls that pounce on scorpions
   and rats twice their size

Owls that signify wisdom and magic
   bring good luck

Owls all but gone from Arizona

Near the Texas border and the Wall
   the last cactus ferruginous pygmy-owls

still cruise
   four and a half feet above the ground.

BLUE DRAGON
(Glaucus atlanticus)

Oh little blue sea dragon,
glaucus atlanticus, you have
so many lovely names:
blue angel, sea swallow,
blue glaucus, dragon slug,

and so does what you live on:
by-the-wind-sailor, purple
sail, little sail or sea raft,
violet snail or purple storm
snail, blue button, blue bottle

jellyfish or Portuguese
man-of-war. Like Afghani
mujahideen, you can swallow
larger predators and keep
their weapons for self-defense.

You store stolen venom in the tips
of your cerata, the feathery
fingerlike things that radiate
from your six appendages
like six tiny headdresses for Cher.

So pretty, so bad. Blue ocean slug,
hermaphroditic, your male
bits extra long and hooked
protect against your mate's
own venomous cerata.

After such hook ups, you
each lay a ribbon of eggs.
Carried by wind and currents,
you float upside-down:
your belly (also your foot,

blue sea slug) blends in
with the water, while your silver-
grey back hides in sunlight
seen from below. If I saw you
collapsed on a beach, a slub

of sea glass, I'd pick you up,
enchanted, and find your poisoned
dart deadlier than a man-of-war's.
No wonder I adore you.
I always had such bad taste in men.

SANTA BARBARA

From the Greek *barbaros,* strange
or foreign, related to barbarian
and barber, from beard. I hoped
I was related to Babar. I hated Barb,

ugly as barbed wire. A verbal jab. I liked
the way the Greeks said *Var-VAR-a!*
and the Chinese cooks at the Nankin sang
Ba-BA-la, in rising then falling tones.

A sort of Rapunzel, locked in a tower:
instead of letting down her hair,
she converted. Her father dragged
her to a Roman magistrate, who cut off

her breasts and paraded her naked
through town. She miraculously healed,
so her father cut off her head. Zapped
by lightning, he was turned to ash.

How Barbara became the patron
saint of explosives: gunners,
miners, mariners, and bandits.
Both a California town and

barbiturates are named for her.
The Church decommissioned her
the year of my bat mitzvah, because
she was a fiction, and she'd rebelled

against her father. But her feast day
had already spread world-wide:
in the Irish artillery corps, she perches
on a cannon like Jane Fonda;

in Germany, geologists hold
Barbarafests. In Santeria, she's merged
with Chango, god of fire and lightning,
thunder and war. In America,

she's ubiquitous, a shape-shifter:
three Barbies sold every second.
More Barbies than guns. No wonder
no one names girls Barbara any more.

PUNK MUPPET
(Mary River Turtle, *Elusor macrurus*)

This unlikely rock star,
with bright green Mohawk
and whiskers of vertical algae,

crazed glass eyes and finger-
like growths beneath its chin,
looks like a troll doll or punk muppet.

Can stay underwater for days
breathing through its cloaca. Just made
the Top Thirty on the EDGE list

of endangered species—because one guy
sold 15,000 eggs to the pet trade,
because these turtles live only

in the Mary River,
and because Australia
has no plan to save them.

Elusor macrurus has long claws
like the godhero
in The Shape of Water.

Might it be saved by weirdness
and good looks? Its plight's
gone viral. What of #1 on the charts,

the Madagascar big-headed turtle,
still being taken for food
and trade? People are hungry.

In China some buy plastic key fobs
with live fish or turtles inside
for good luck. Some buy them

just to set the tiny captives free.

CALLING BLUE WHALES
(*Balaenoptera musculus*)

Melville used the sailors' term, Sulphur Bottom:

seldom seen   never chased
  would run away with rope-walks of line
    Prodigies are told of him
    I can say nothing more that is true
nor can the oldest Nantucketer.

Blue Whale

from Norwegian *blahval*
  named by Svend Foyn
    inventor of the exploding harpoon gun—
  A century later
they were all but gone.

Balaenoptera musculus

Musculus means
  muscle or little mouse
    (a joke by Linnaeus?) So
  enormous, we can weigh
blue whales only cut in pieces.

Suborder: *Mysticeti*

We do not know
  the true nature of the entity
    we are destroying.
   They swim in pairs,
breeding grounds unknown.

Ancient sea monsters

No predators
   but ship crash and sonar,
     drilling and plastic, our toxins
   concentrated in their rich milk
poisoning their first-born.

Leviathan

whose deep rumblings travel hundreds of miles
   underwater, so low we feel as much as hear them,
     four-note songs like humpback whales'.
   No one knows what they're singing,
maybe warnings, elegies, calling one another's names.

REFUGE AT DEPTH

1. Rhinochimaera
    (Rhinochimaera africana, atlantica, & pacifica)

Chimaeras (marine monsters in Greek)
  have the best names—
    spookfish, rabbit fish, ghost shark,

rat fish. Rhinochimaera adds Greek
  for nose—spearnose,
    paddlenose, straightnose, knifenose.

Streamlined like their nearest kin, sharks, but
  oviparous and
    more ethereal, rhino-

chimaera find refuge at depth
  beyond our nets.
    Weirder than aliens—like

the lovechild of Dumbo and a shark,
  one swims ghost-white
    out of the black ocean depths,

appearing to fly through a night sky
  with elegant
    black-edged fins flapping like wings,

huge dark eyes and long conical snout
  up-curled, feeling
    for fish, a sensitive trunk—

What do we know? they emerge from and
  return to Earth's
    strange and ever-teeming womb.

2. Dumbo Octopus
    (Grimpotheutis)

Dumbos are bellshaped, semi-
translucent, with huge eyes
and fins like elephant ears
they flap to move
with peculiar grace,

or hover above the deep
sea floor, resembling
small umbrellas. Startled,
they invert like
umbrellas blown inside out.

Also called winged octopus
or jellyheads, Dumbos
live in the abyssal depths.
The deep so vast
and Dumbos so rare, she's

always ready, with eggs at
various stages. If
she gets lucky, he gives her
a sperm packet
to stash until she's safe.

Newborn, octopuses can
fend off killer whales and
sharks. Intelligent, they sleep
like us, dream and
learn. Dumbos see only

bioluminescence. When
our latest craft descend
to their depths, can they even
perceive us? They're
not threatened by us. Yet.

MADAGASCAN MOON MOTH
(Argemma mittrei)

He has only a handful of nights
to find her. She barely moves
from her loose, silver silk cocoon.
She hangs to dry her gold velvet wings,

her eggs good just for a day.
He must move fast, evading bats,
to win one endless day of copulation
so she can lay her hundred eggs and die.

Most will feed birds, but the few caterpillars
who survive munch nonstop for months,
molt their chitin skin four times before,
fat and bright green, they spin

their moonlike cocoons (cratered with holes
for the rain to run through) where they'll sleep
half their life away, while changing into
their splendid final dress.

Wings a golden hand-span, edged black
as burnt toast, their russet scallops
and purple eyespots work as camou-
flage in the remnant rainforest.

They do not eat. They live for a week
off the fat stored in their gold-furred bodies.
His feathery antennae can pick up
her pheromones from miles away.

In the Madagascan night, she silently
summons a trembling male, who vibrates
his brave body and wings to warm himself
for takeoff in the cold highlands.

To distract bats, he spins his extravagant
and expendable long red tail. They aim for that
and miss him as he burns through the dark,
improbable and fleeting, the Comet Moth.

EL ZUNZUNCITO (CUBAN BEE HUMMINGBIRD)
(*Mellisuga helenae*)

> ...*there always exists one more beyond in the marvelous works of creation.*
> —Juan Lembeye, *Los aves de la isla de Cuba,* 1850.

The smallest bird lives on nectar.
   Named *zunzun* for the whir

of its wings, which
   invisibly trace infinity.

Also *zumbite* (buzzer)
   or *trovador* (troubadour).

Co-evolved with flowers,
   lime to sapphire,

they can mate shimmering in mid-air.
   In spring *el macho's*

head and neck grow brilliant
   pink-orange-reds. He joins

a lek, a band or team
   that sings and competes in

intricate displays, in hoodies
   like iridescent lipsticks.

Each female a prom queen
   can hook up

with several *machos*.
   She'll still end up a single mom.

Fed on orchids and sarsaparilla,
   she builds her cup-shaped nest alone

(so tiny, it can fit on a clothespin)
   in calabash or cashew tree.

She gathers wool from ceiba
   trees or twisted airplant,

lined with moss, down, fur.
   Spider web for spandex.

She lays two eggs like white
   coffee beans. Her blue-green

plumage blends in; *el macho*'s
   gaud could give away the nest

to hawks, falcons, even
   spiders. The chicks

hatch blind: naked red
   turns to gold, then dull

velvet with a cobalt sheen.
   For protein, she hunts

mosquitoes the way hawks
   do pigeons, thousands a day

till the two-inch
   pichones have fledged.

Back on her liquid diet
   (she weighs less than a dime)

she sips a thousand blossoms
   a day of hummingbird or fire

bush, cup of gold or chalice
　　vine. Birds so beautiful

in the nineteenth century rich women
　　wore them, stuffed, on their hats.

22 EXTINCTIONS IN 2021

These mussels had secrets that we'll never know:

the flat pigtoe
  upland combshell
    stirrupshell &
      Southern acornshell

    pearly mussels: green-blossom
      tubercled-blossom
        turgid-blossom &
      yellow-blossom

done in by dams. By us & rats & mosquitoes

11 birds, mostly Hawaiian—
  the Kauai akialoa, nukupu'u,
    O'o and large Kauai thrush,
      the Maui akepa & nunupu'u,
        the Molokai creeper & Po'ouli—

    the bridled white-eye bird,
      ivory-billed woodpecker
        & Bachman's warbler.

11 birds, 8 mussels, 2 fish & 1 bat,
  the Little Mariana fruit bat.

We don't fully understand what we lost.

While the bombs rain on Ukraine
  why do I mourn these small
    shapes by most of us unseen
      silently filtering streams
        or pollinating blossoms?

Their lost songs and ingenious forms
  will never again grace air or water.
    They were our little sisters and brothers
      whether we ever met or called their names.

LONESOMEST GEORGE
(*Achatinella apexfulva*)

How to sing the loneliness of George,
last of his kind, bred and dead in a lab
in Hawaii, extinction capital of the world?

*Hawaii was the most magical place
on Earth, with beautiful, rainbow-colored
snails hanging from the trees.*

We've all broken down and cried in the field,
said David, the last to see 20 kinds
in the wild. He started the love shack,

a captive breeding program in a trailer
where George ended his days
alone in his terrarium, among

2,000 other snails on the brink.
Hermaphroditic, some snails
can reproduce solo, but not George.

A hermit who rarely emerged
from his shell. What for?
No forest, no one to mate with,

14 years in solitary till he died of old age.

Named for Lonesome George,
the last Pinta Island tortoise.

In native legend, tree snails are revered
as the voice of the forest. No one now

can remember how they sound.

BETTER NAMES FOR POLAR BEARS

In Old Norse they're called White Sea Deer,
Rider of Icebergs, The Seal's Dread, The Whale's
Bane, Sailor of the Floe. Sea Bear, *Ursus
Maritimus* in Latin, *Thalactos* in Greek.

Ice Bear, *Isbjorn*, in Norway and Denmark,
The White Bear in Russia, *Beliy Medved*.
Animal Worthy of Great Respect,
Nanuk, among the Inuit, and
Ever-Wandering One, *Pihoqahiak*.

Grandfather, *Gyp*, or Stepfather, *Orqoi*,
to the Ket of Siberia. In Greenland,
Master of Helping Spirits, *Tornassuk*.
The Old Man in the Fur Cloak, to
the Sami of Lapland. Also, God's Dog.

STONE SOUP
(Anostraca)

Who, if his son asks for bread, would give him
a stone? Maybe the father of the fairy shrimp:
three hundred species, from Antarctica
to desert to frozen mountain lakes.
Some have no fathers—parthenogenesis.
All can go dormant: in diapause, as cysts,
they can withstand drought, frost, salt,
radiation, even the vacuum of space,
for centuries—then, carried by currents
or predators or wind, stirred back to life
by the ephemeral waters of spring pools
all over the Midwest, they cruise, supping
on algae soup, feeding mallards and fish.
Who needs any more miracle than this?

WATER STRIDER
    (Gerridae)

Late, you swim along the lake's eastern shore.
Low sun glances off the dancing surface,
ripples silver across gray bark and wavers
over the hemlocks like green-gold smoke.

Do your strokes disturb the current, casting
these intricate patterns as on a screen?
Or would light and water weave just the same
if no one were here to see? You can't know.

You glide by, steadily and slow, watching
what seems to be the work of your own hands—
you think you are the star of this
ephemeral light-show. But you will never
be sure you're not just a water strider
skimming past without leaving a trace…

THE LAST JAGUAR
(Panthera onca)

Schoolkids in Tuscon named
                         the last jaguar standing
El Jefe
       The Boss.
             He prowls
                    the Santa Rita Mountains
an immigrant
          from the Sierra Madre.

The last jaguar before him
                 Macho B
lured with female scat
                 killed in a botch-job in 2009.

The last jaguar in Texas
                 shot in 1948, the last
female jaguar in the US
                 shot the same year as JFK.

The Jaguar God of the Night
                   Lord of the Underworld.

In Mexican Spanish
            the jaguar is *el tigre*.
                              Jaguar comes
from the native *yaguar*
             he who kills with one leap.

Jaguars avoid
                and rarely attack us.
Solitary.
        Elusive.
                Their rosettes help them
disappear
        in dappled
                deep-forest light.
     Hard to spot
                let alone count.

El Jefe can be known
                by his unique coat.

Where jaguars once roamed
                the Southwest freely
        El Jefe hunts alone.

                The Wall
would keep females out,
                dooming El Jefe
                        to be the very last.

The Ese Ejja
        People of the Amazon say
                The Jaguar
only shows himself to you
                when you are ready to see him.

III.
SACRED SHARDS

RESOLUTIONS FOR 2024

Let go of worrying.

Practice daily levitation.
Say goodbye to time.

Learn the language of animals.

Become carbon neutral.
Forgive your ex-husbands.

Embrace death with your whole

heart, as Lao Tsu teaches.
Taste like a peach.

Sweep the footprints off the moon.

STAR APPLE

any way you slice it
inside each apple a star
around seeds black as holes

from which a tree might
root branch leaf and bloom
as Kabbalah's tree of life blows

from *a spark*
of impenetrable darkness
at the center of each galaxy

a black hole unknowable
as the growing universe
mostly dark energy

inexplicable as the fruit
that fell for Newton
as for Eve

any way you slice it
stars fall from apples
holes seed our sky

as the tongue loves
the apple does the night
sky love the star

AP PHYSICS

> *One can never protect a single human being from any kind*
> *of suffering. That's what makes one so tremendously weary.*
> —Mrs. Armfeld in *Smiles of a Summer Night*

Your son says, Did you know
you exert a gravitational pull
on everything in the universe
and everything in the universe
exerts a gravitational pull
on you?
        And that's what makes you
so tremendously weary,
you think, until you learn
there's no such thing
as gravity but rather space-
time curves like a stretchy
fabric and things roll towards
one another like balls that follow
grooved tracks around an incline

and then again that Einstein
was wrong: there is no time
or space at the tiniest
level, just quanta weaving
the net of what is, though
these are but crude metaphors

as you know from fasting,
eating peyote or giving birth
but which, to survive on the gross
scale of a body, you must forget.

And this, too, makes you
tremendously weary, or perhaps
it's just motherhood and age,
which also don't really exist.

ON TEACHING HOMER FOR THIRTY YEARS

Athena's turned Odysseus into a bum again,
withering his handsome body arthritic,
dimming his fine bright eyes, dulling his hair,
turning his clothes to rags. I want to cry,

That's just what it's like! I'm really
a hip fresh-person like you, slightly bored
by this slog, suffering a temporary
transformation, expecting in each mirror

my real face—stunned anew like the poor crew
to see boar bristles sprouting from the chin,
awaiting Circe's magic wand to switch me
back. That's exactly what it's like, I want

to cry, but don't. The class could not care less.
Like Telemachus, they will never grow old.

HOW TO AGE GRACEFULLY

You may think sweater set, but you must never, ever wear one.
—Kate Moss

When you kvetch,
your son says, *Go
out in the Adirondacks
and get eaten by a wild animal.*

When X-rays show your bones
vanishing, imagine your
latter years in a wheelchair,
brilliant as Stephen Hawking.

Your son, a blooming
rose of muscle, says,
*No makeup. It just
makes you look worse.*

Remember how you used
to admire Aunt Clara's
concentric smile wrinkles,
her raconteur's contralto?

What to wear? He suggests
you dress like Bolivian women
in their colorful ponchos
that cover everything.

When you despair,
he offers to push you
out on an ice floe
for the polar bears.

FABLE

At the end of your childhood, birds came.
To magnify the looming empty nest,
they built all around our yard and home.

Wrens in the birdhouse, bluebirds the same,
chickadees in the mailbox, noisy guests.
At the end of your childhood, birds came

to show how swiftly you'd be gone,
and yet how every fledgling is blessed.
They nested all around our yard and home—

robins, finches, I don't know all their names—
singing before dawn, till I lay down to rest.
At the end of your childhood, birds came.

Soon you'll try your wings and start to roam
the way I flew off, so young, into the west,
forgetting the nest in the yard back home.

Before you hatched I knew, once you were grown,
I would have to ace love's hardest test.
At the end of your childhood, birds came
to fill the emptiness with singing. Home.

WILD LIFE

Go out to scatter bread crumbs
for the birds, see the snout
of a polar bear sticking
out of the snow—I'm standing

on its back! and there's another
beside it, and another—
seven in a row, no,
three rows of seven—

twenty-one polar bears
tucked under the snow
asleep side by side
filling the whole back yard

like blintzes in a pan
or stepping stones
I could hop across
to the end of the world

APRIL JOURNAL

My father would have turned 100 today.

Sometimes I'm glad he's not here
to witness. At others, I feel him in each
cell, closer than when he was alive.

A young sperm whale washed up

near a lighthouse in Cabo de Palos,
sixty-four pounds of garbage in its gut—
trashbags, fishing net, ropes, and a drum.

Each spring now the saddest on record.

Another day in the march of ecocide,
Sam Hamill used to post.
People mostly made no remark.

In India, birds fell dead from the sky.

Would you light yourself on fire
like Wynn Bruce on Earth Day
before the Supreme Court?

Thich Quang Duc set himself on fire

on TV again. He sits utterly still,
does not cry out, certain
of rebirth as we were of gravity.

That torch keeps burning.

I am breathing in
and contemplating letting go.
I am breathing out

and contemplating letting go.

Though living in the end days
with thirteen kinds of crazy,
still some birds return, one by one.

THE OWL GUY

Good news! There are men
who stop for wounded owls
track them into the woods
cradle them in their Carhartt jackets
till the wildlife guy arrives.

After a 12-hour shift, Chance
was driving home, bone-tired at 6 a.m.—
no time to brake for the hurt owl, miraculously
centered between the pickup's wheels.

Chance said, *I'm the owl guy at work now.*

Rehabbed and released three weeks later,
the barred owl ignored his *What's up, buddy?*
and soared out of that Walmart parking lot
to reclaim its realm of sky over Waterford.

MINNESOTA DREAMING

At the end of the line
(I must have drifted off)
I have a suitcase full of sand

I empty into the aisle
of the deserted car.
On his final pass

the conductor drops
a handful of sand
down my back.

You were to meet me
here in Oconomowoc
on a different train

—I can't work
this new cell phone—
Are you there? Once

I filled a suitcase with water
but by the time my father
dropped me off

at the Art Institute
it had all drained out the trunk
of the blue Oldsmobile.

When he said I'm nothing
but a grain of sand he was
nearing the end of the line.

CRUISING FOR SENIORS
(from *Cruising for Seniors* by Paul H. Keller)

your cruising life will be one of terror
get another spouse
or give up your dream

all over the world are women looking for skippers
and skippers looking for women
the keel can fall off

abandoning ship do not waste time
on your wedding ring   look around
remember   safety is a state of mind

most men found floating
face down in the sea
had their flies open

learning celestial navigation
what should you watch for
read the stars wind waves

   red at night
   sailors delight
a coconut waits on every tree

be safe and have fun
carry lubricant
get help

stroke is such an apt name   isn't it
you lose a little control
why all this fuss

many are bolts from the blue
finally you will bless the day
sometimes drinking helps

a cruiser is a vagabond
at one with sea and sky and stars
are you ready to cast off

for that great adventure
death follows rapidly
halos may appear

NEW YEAR'S DAY

Listening to Bach
at the Troy Music Hall,
the air ringing bright,
you closed your eyes
until roused by urgent
stage whispers, *Jay! Jay!*
We've got to get you out of here!

You opened them to see
the old gent in front of you
being hustled out by his wife
and two ushers. As once
your young husband
blindfolded you,
bundled you into a cab,

led you by the hand into a sound-
scape you sensed like a bat—
vast, circling, sublime—
revealed to be an orchestra
tuning up in Carnegie Hall.
You closed your eyes again
to keep hearing in 3-D—

like the famous acoustics
of the Troy Music Hall.
What happened to Jay
you'll never know, but
what a way to go—swooping
from the heights of a Brandenburg
Concerto back into the dark.

WORRY / DON'T WORRY

I don't worry about the universe expanding—
        an exhalation of dark matter,
                the Secret One slowly growing a body,

or our galaxy,
        a white cat stretched
                across black sheets.

Don't worry about the solar system,
        though our sun will burn out like any furnace,

or our planet that can scrape us off like mold,
        wash away our trash in a few million years
                and mix up some new concoctions.

I do worry about our paranoid-
        schizophrenic States, though not
                about upstate, so far
                        from fire and floods, so far.

Don't worry about this little house
        that's withstood the rain
                of three centuries.

I worry about taxes, exes,
        this plague or the next
                or eventual dementia.

Don't worry about the microscopic life
        streaming in warm currents up my legs
                and trunk into my nose

or about my cells
        despite the spiked invader,
                the bats' revenge.

Never worry about my ten octillion atoms,
    my quarks and leptons
        doing their quantum Lindy.

I don't worry about the mostly empty space
    inside or out,
        just that infinitesimal

crosshair of infinity
    where the loops
        of the sideways eight meet,

my particular X-marks-the-spot
    or black dot
        on the lottery ticket.

UKIYO-E

I go to bed with shutters open
watch the snow
swirling in streetlight

The sudden apparition
of a face
in my upstairs window

An Utamaro woodblock print
of a geisha combing her hair
hangs over my bed

Reflected in dark glass
she seems to move
a hologram

outside in the storm
snow driving through her
streaming hair she floats

riding the wind
a lost ghost
from some Noh play

eerily beautiful
ukiyo-e
the floating world

where she once lived

where we all
briefly
appear

DREAM VOICE

In a mirror, you see
your human shape, swathed

in black lace, translucent
and pulsing like a jellyfish,

heart and womb shining
through like the Visible

Woman's, wondrous as
the Piglet octopus

with its crown of tentacles
and saucer eyes, or

the pocket shark shaped
like a palm-sized sperm whale,

the caterpillar fringed
like a Mardi Gras float

or Uncle Walt marveling
at how his ankles bend.

Never worry about beauty again
a voice says. *You too*

are the Nameless in drag.

THOUGHT CLOUD

Thank God, they cannot cut down the clouds!
      —Thoreau

The clouds are not cotton batting in the jewel case of the stars.

The clouds are not swimmers in the stratosphere.

The clouds are not the sledges of the gods.

The clouds are not charging dragons

      or sharks with open jaws.

The clouds are not harbingers or symbols.

The clouds are not old dreams of Turner.

The clouds are not children shrieking Marco! Polo!

The clouds are not drones hovering above impoverished villages.

The clouds are not the braille of angels.

That one is not a baboon turning into a crab.

The clouds are not airships

      though they may resemble the petitions of illiterate sailors.

The clouds are not striving or competitive.

That one is not shaped like a penis,

      or not for long, anyway.

The clouds are not endangered. Or invasive.

The clouds are not the longing of refugees in cages

        or camps, though clouds may be the only beauty visible there.

The clouds are not doodles of the dead.

They're our single stream of tears recycled

        and reincarnated fields of snow.

They are not translatable.

They can not stay.

NOTES

The sources for many of these poems are the EDGE Lists of Evolutionarily Distinct and Globally Endangered species.

"Luck" is inspired by Layli Long Soldier's poem "38."

"Average Monkey" ends with a quote from Mu Soeng's book on The Heart Sutra.

"Weight" is inspired by "The biomass distribution on Earth," Yinon M. Bar-On, Rob Phillips, and Ron Milo, *PNAS (Proceedings of the National Academy of Sciences of the United States)*, June 19, 2018.

"Calling Blue Whales" quotes Herman Melville and Arthur C. Clarke.

"Star Apple" quotes the Zohar, a central text of Kabbalah.

"The Owl Guy" is from "Rescued owl returns to sky over Waterford," *Albany Times Union*, January 2, 2019.

"Cruising for Seniors" is a found poem from *Cruising for Seniors* by Paul H. Keller.

"Worry / Don't Worry" quotes a line from *The Kabir Book* by Robert Bly.

"Dream Voice" refers to Whitman's "Song of Myself" and Ram Dass.

ABOUT THE AUTHOR

Barbara Ungar's prior book, *Save Our Ship*, won the Snyder Publication Prize from Ashland Poetry Press and a Franklin Award from the Independent Book Publishers Association, and was a Distinguished Favorite at the Independent Press Awards. Earlier books include *Charlotte Brontë, You Ruined My Life* and *Immortal Medusa*, both Hilary Tham Capital Collection selections from The Word Works, and *The Origin of the Milky Way*, which won the Gival Prize and an Eric Hoffer Award. Her work has been translated into Italian, Spanish, Portuguese, and Bulgarian. The Standish Chair in English at The College of Saint Rose, she lives in Saratoga Springs, New York.

barbaraungar.net

ABOUT THE ARTIST

Joseph Cornell (1903-1972), American assemblage artist, was best known for his "memory boxes" or "poetic theaters," in which he arranged old photos, Victorian bric-a-brac, dime-store trinkets, and ephemera from the used bookstores and thrift shops of New York City. He also made experimental films and flat collages from the dossiers he kept on his obsessions, including ballerinas and actresses such as Jackie Lane. Famously reclusive, he lived most of his life on Utopia Parkway in Flushing, Queens, caring for his mother and handicapped younger brother. Self-taught, Cornell became highly acclaimed, with work in museum collections worldwide. His last show was for children, with boxes displayed at child height, and refreshments of brownies and cherry soda.

ABOUT THE WORD WORKS

Since its founding in 1974, The Word Works has published volumes of contemporary poetry and presented public programs. Its imprints include The Washington Prize, The Tenth Gate Prize, The Hilary Tham Capital Collection, and International Editions.

Monthly, The Word Works offers free programs in its Café Muse Literary Salon. Winners of the Jacklyn Potter Young Poets Competition are presented in the June Café Muse program.

As a 501(c)3 organization, The Word Works has received awards from the National Endowment for the Arts, the National Endowment for the Humanities, the D.C. Commission on the Arts & Humanities, the Witter Bynner Foundation, Poets & Writers, The Writer's Center, Bell Atlantic, the David G. Taft Foundation, and others, including many generous private patrons.

An archive of artistic and administrative materials in the Washington Writing Archive is housed in the George Washington University Gelman Library. The Word Works is a member of the Community of Literary Magazines and Presses and its books are distributed by Small Press Distribution.

wordworksbooks.org

OTHER WORD WORKS BOOKS

Annik Adey-Babinski, *Okay Cool No Smoking Love Pony*
Karren L. Alenier, *From the Belly: Poets Respond to Gerturude Stein's Tender Buttons*
Karren L. Alenier, *Wandering on the Outside*
Nathalie Anderson, *Rough*
Emily August, *The Punishments Must Be a School*
Jennifer Barber, *The Sliding Boat Our Bodies Made*
Andrea Carter Brown, *September 12*
Willa Carroll, *Nerve Chorus*
Grace Cavalieri, *Creature Comforts / The Long Game: Poems Selected & New*
Abby Chew, *A Bear Approaches from the Sky*
Nadia Colburn, *The High Shelf*
Henry Crawford, *The Binary Planet*
Barbara Goldberg, *Berta Broadfoot and Pepin the Short / Breaking & Entering: New and Selected Poems*
Akua Lezli Hope, *Them Gone*
Michael Klein, *The Early Minutes of Without: Poems Selected & New*
Deborah Kuan, *Women on the Moon*
Frannie Lindsay, *If Mercy*
Elaine Magarrell, *The Madness of Chefs*
Chloe Martinez, *Ten Thousand Selves*
Marilyn McCabe, *Glass Factory*
JoAnne McFarland, *Identifying the Body*
Leslie McGrath, *Feminists Are Passing from Our Lives*
Kevin McLellan, *Ornitheology*
Ron Mohring, *The Boy Who Reads in the Trees*
A. Molotkov, *Future Symptoms*
Ann Pelletier, *Letter That Never*
W.T. Pfefferle, *My Coolest Shirt*
Ayaz Pirani, *Happy You Are Here*
Robert Sargent, *Aspects of a Southern Story / A Woman from Memphis*
Roger Smith, *Radiation Machine Gun Funk*
Jeddie Sophonius, *Love & Sambal*
Julia Story, *Spinster for Hire*
Cheryl Clark Vermeulen, *They Can Take It Out*
Julie Marie Wade, *Skirted*
Miles Waggener, *Superstition Freeway*
Fritz Ward, *Tsunami Diorama*
Camille-Yvette Welsch, *The Four Ugliest Children in Christendom*
Amber West, *Hen & God*
Maceo Whitaker, *Narco Farm*

www.ingramcontent.com/pod-product-compliance
Lightning Source LLC
Chambersburg PA
CBHW020729100426
42735CB00038B/1102